The Good Music Trivia Book

by Mel Simons

ALSO BY MEL SIMONS:

The Old-Time Radio Trivia Book

The Old-Time Television Trivia Book

Old-Time Radio Memories

The Show-Biz Trivia Book

Old-Time Television Memories

The Movie Trivia Book

Voices from the Philco

The Good Music Trivia Book

by Mel Simons

BearManor Media
2012

The Good Music Trivia Book

© 2012 Mel Simons

For information, address:

BearManor Media
P. O. Box 71426
Albany, GA 31708

bearmanormedia.com

Typesetting and layout by John Teehan

Published in the USA by BearManor Media

ISBN — 1-59393-694-X
978-1-59393-694-5

Dedication

*This book is dedicated to two
of my favorite fraternity brothers
from Emerson College,
Dick Lefebvre and Bob Greenman*

Mel Simons and Patti Page

Foreword

One day not too long ago I was driving along Route 101 near my home in San Diego, CA and I heard a thump, thump, thump. At first I thought something happened to my car but it got louder and kept a regular beat. At the next light another car pulled up on my right side and the noise coming from it was almost unbearable. I just shook my head and thought this is what they call music these days. Whatever happened to the "good music" we have known for so many years?

Those of us who are now considered senior citizens have good memories of Doris Day, Frankie Laine, Andy Williams, my dear friend Rosemary Clooney, all the Big Bands, and many others. Their music had significance. It meant something to all of us. Where we were, what we were doing or who we were with when we listened to their songs. Perhaps some will remember a few of my songs too. That is what I hear most when traveling around the world for concerts or other appearances. Fans always thank me for the "good music" I've been proud to sing throughout my career. They have called me a "territory singer" because several of my songs touched the hearts of people in different geographical areas, for example, "Old Cape Cod," "Allegheny Moon" or "Tennessee Waltz".

Mel Simons' newest book "The Good Music Trivia Book" is a wonderful compilation of facts and information written by a man whose life's mission is to entertain. He is a master at it. This book is jammed packed with fun-filled quizzes that are truly entertaining and helped remind me of good times and good friends. There were even a couple of questions that got me stumped.

What is Barbra Streisand's' middle name anyway?

Good music has been an important part of m life. It helped me celebrate good times and got me through some of the most difficult times. As I shared *The Good Music Trivia Book* with some friends, it has already brought joy and laughter into our lives. I hope it will do the same for each of you.

– Patti Page

Preface

"They just don't write songs like these anymore!"

How many times have you heard that expression?

Good Music means different things to different people.

To me, it is the music that is melodic and hummable, and the songs with lyrics you can sing-a-long to because they make sense.

I loved and still love those tunes, and I greatly admire the singers and musicians who made those songs pop music standards. These are the songs you played on the juke box in your favorite soda fountain "joints," that wonderful music-playing device that was so much more satisfying than the current CD players and iPods.

The Good Music Trivia Book will make you smile and want to burst into song. At the same time, you will get the chance to see how well you remember the great music, the songs, the singers and the bandleaders of yesteryear.

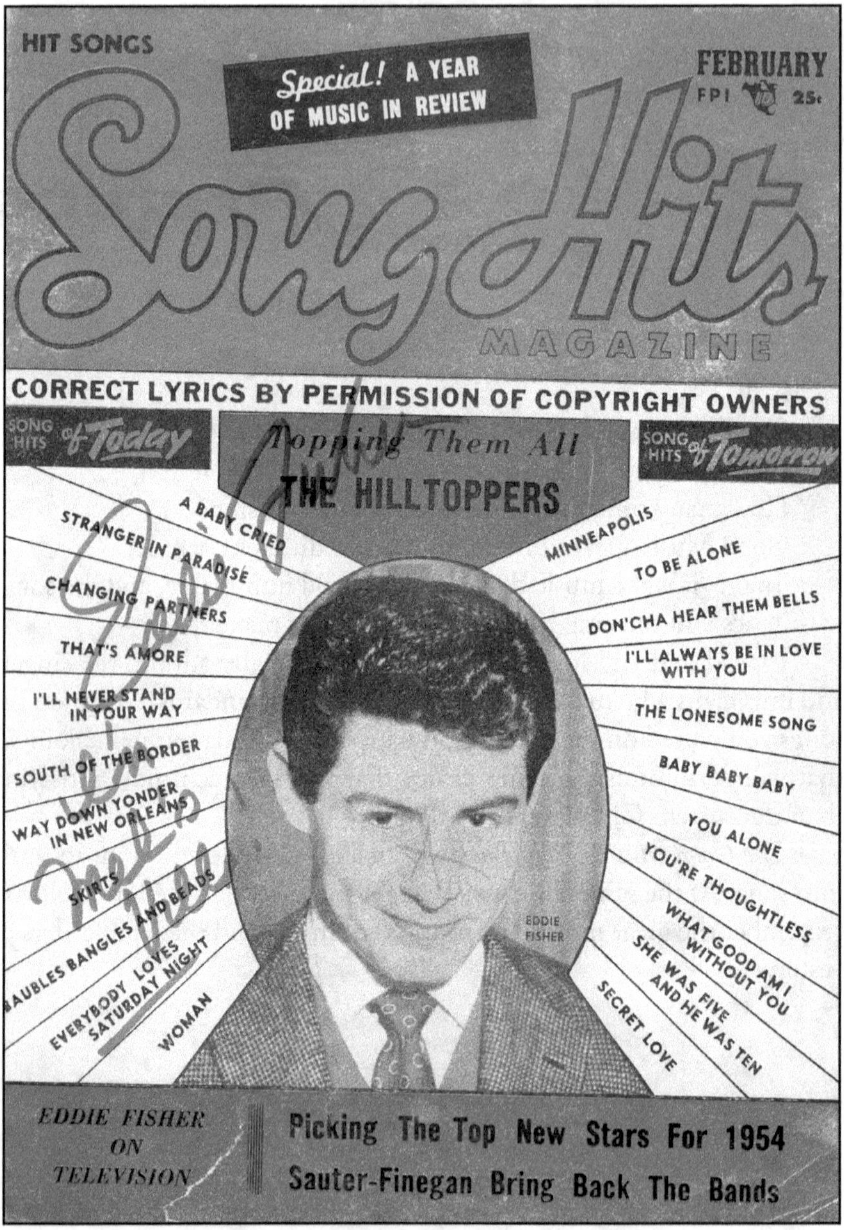

Eddie Fisher

Quiz #1

EDDIE FISHER
(Answers on page 107)

1. Eddie was the production singer at what well known night club?

2. He sang with Eddie Ashman's Orchestra at what Catskill Mountain Resort?

3. What famous entertainer discovered Eddie at this resort?

4. Name Eddie's television show.

5. Name Eddie's first three wives.

6. All of his hits were on what record label?

7. What was his first hit record?

8. What was his first number one record?

9. His biggest selling record was number one for eight weeks. Name that song.

10. Name his hit record from the move *White Christmas.*

Eddie Fisher

Quiz #2

ONE HIT WONDERS

Match the singers with their only hit record
(Answers on Page 107)

1. "Tip-Toe Thru the Tulips"
2. "Cry Me a River"
3. "Hello Walls"
4. "Pink Shoe Laces"
5. "The Men in My Little Girl's Life"
6. "The Breeze and I"
7. "Short People"
8. "He's Got the Whole World in His Hands"
9. "Paper Roses"
10. "We'll Sing In The Sunshine"

a. Marie Osmond
b. Mike Douglas
c. Dodie Stevens
d. Tiny Tim
e. Laurie London
f. Julie London
g. Faron Young
h. Randy Newman
i. Caterina Valente
j. Gale Garnett

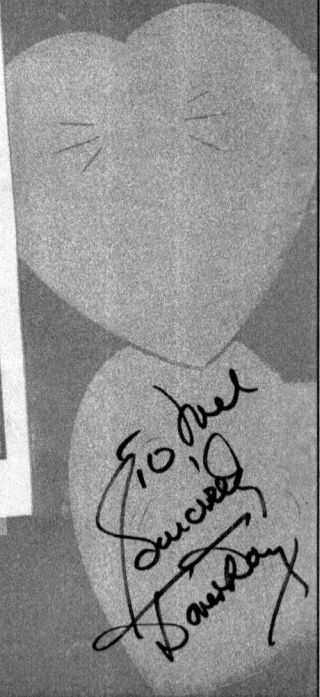

Doris Day

Quiz #3

GENERAL QUESTIONS
(Answers on Page 108)

1. Name the long-time host of *American Bandstand*.

2. Who was known as "The King of Swing?"

3. Name the #1 song that Doris Day had, from the movie: *Calamity Jane*.

4. What instrument did Connie Francis play as a youngster?

5. Tony Williams was the lead singer of what group?

6. Name the four Ames Brothers.

7. Who wrote *Rhapsody In Blue*?

8. What was Kate Smith's biggest selling record?

9. Simon and Garfunkle sang the song "Mrs. Robinson" in what movie?

10. Who was Herb Alpert's partner with A & M Records?

Connie Francis

Quiz #4

SONGS

Fill in the number
(Answers on Page 108)

1. "_____ Coins, in the Fountain"

2. "When You Were Sweet _____ "

3. "_____ Trombones Led the Big Parade"

4. "Beat Me Daddy, _____ to the Bar"

5. "_____ Lessons from Madame LaZonga"

6. "Tea for _____ "

7. "_____ Cents a Dance"

8. "_____ Little Indian Boys

9. "Give Me _____ Minutes More"

10. "_____ Singular Sensation"

The Ames Bros.

Quiz #5

VOCAL GROUPS

What group had these hit records?
(Answers on Page 108)

1. "All I Have to Do Is Dream"
2. "One Less Bell to Answer"
3. "When I Fall in Love"
4. "26 Miles"
5. "Sherry"
6. "Graduation Day"
7. "No More"
8. "Sh-Boom"
9. "Twilight Time"
10. "I See the Moon"

a. The Four Preps
b. The Everly Brothers
c. The DeJohn Sisters
d. The Platters
e. The Mariners
f. The Fifth Dimension
g. The Four Seasons
h. The Lettermen
i. The Crew-Cuts
j. The Rover Boys

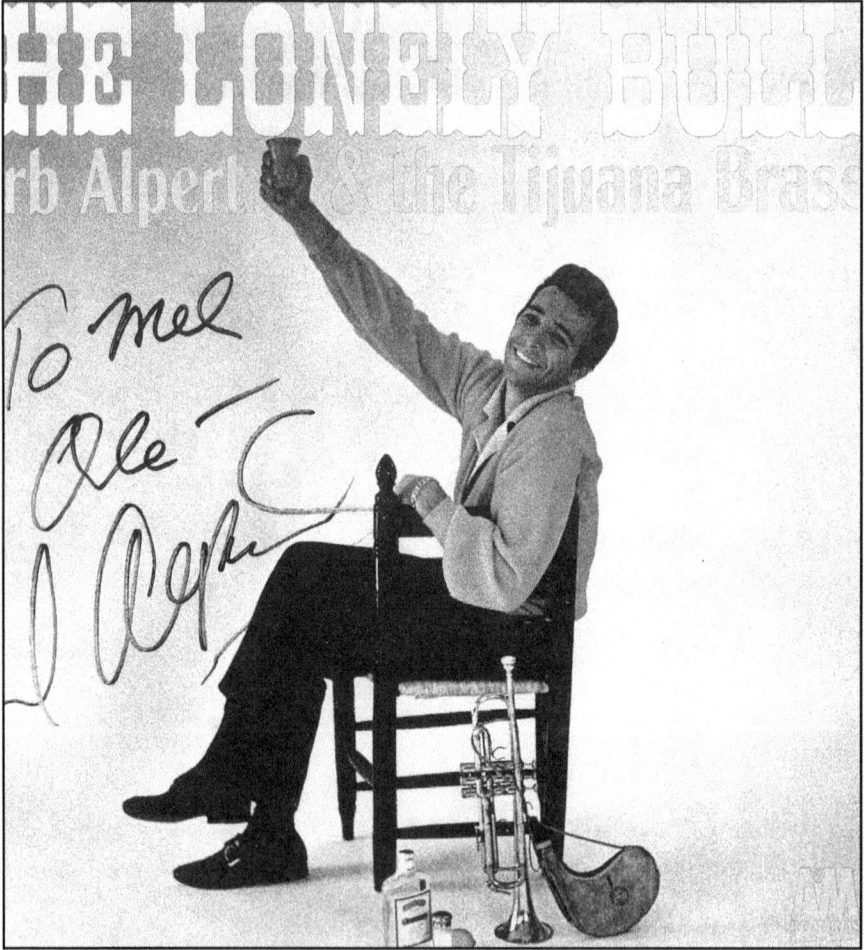

Herb Alptert

Quiz #6

SINGING COMMERCIALS

Fill in the product
(Answers on Page 109)

1. Hot Dogs, _____ Hot Dogs. The dogs kids love to bite

2. Candy coated popcorn, peanuts, and a prize. That's what you get in _____ _____

3. Plop, plop, fizz, fizz, oh what a relief it is _____ _____

4. Double your pleasure, double your fun, with double good, double good, _____ _____ gum

5. You can trust your car, to the man who wears the star. The big, bright _____ star

6. Sometimes I feel like a nut, sometimes I don't, _____ _____ got nuts, _____ don't

7. Come alive, you're in the _____ generation

8. _____ _____ __ '_____ is that heavenly coffee. Better coffee a millionaire's money can't buy

9. _____-_____-_____ the San Francisco treat. _____-_____-_____ its flavor can't be beat

10. ………And _____ does it best

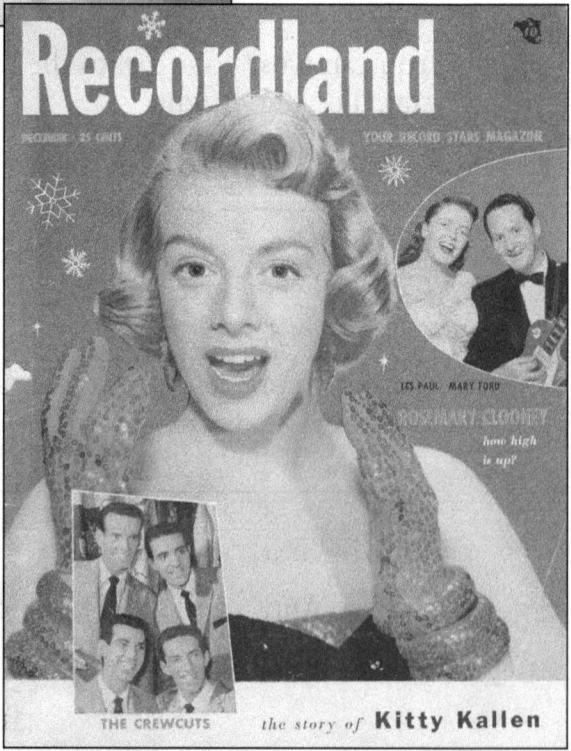

Rosemary Clooney

Quiz #7

ROSEMARY CLOONEY
(Answers on Page 109)

1. Rosie sang with what big band?

2. She often sang with her sister. What was her sister's name?

3. Who brought her to Columbia records?

4. She sang a duet with Guy Mitchell on her first record. Name the Song.

5. What was her first number one record?

6. She had a two-sided number one record. Name both songs.

7. Name her hit record that was a Mambo.

8. Rosie did a series of radio show with what famous singer?

9. Name the singer that is Rosie's daughter-in-law.

10. She co-starred in what well known holiday movie?

Benny Goodman

Artie Shaw

Quiz #8

TWO GREAT CLARINET PLAYERS

Is it Benny Goodman or Artie Shaw?
(Answers on Page 109)

1. Who was known as "The King Of Swing"?

2. Peggy Lee sang with which band?

3. Who was born in New York and grew up in Connecticut?

4. Who was once married to Ava Gardner?

5. Buddy Rich played drums for whose band?

6. Who was famous for a Carnegie Hall concert?

7. Harry James played trumpet for whose band?

8. Ziggy Elman played trumpet for whose band?

9. Who was known for "The Gramercy Five?"

10. Who had the hit record "Frenesi"?

Merv Griffen

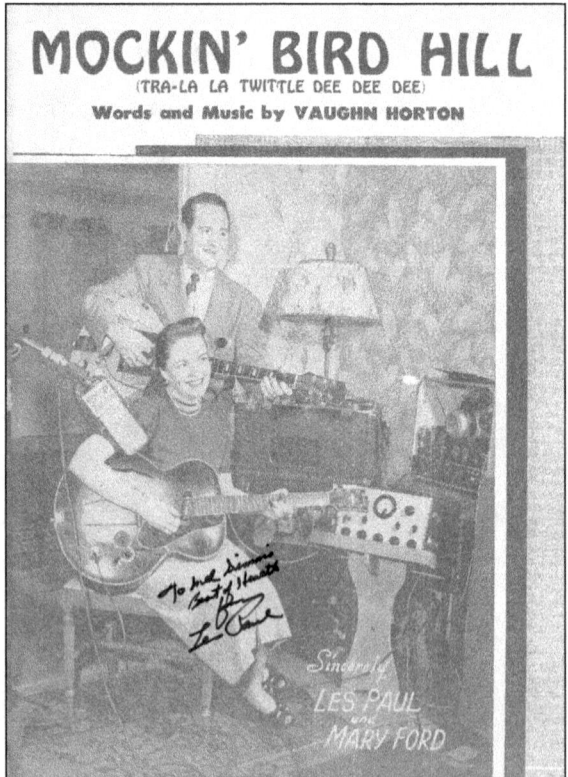

Les Paul and Mary Ford

Quiz #9

GENERAL QUESTIONS
(Answers on Page 110)

1. Who started The Chipmunks?

2. Merv Griffin sang with what orchestra?

3. Sammy Davis, Jr. had one number one record. What was it?

4. Frankie Laine sang the theme of what television western?

5. Al Alberts was the original lead singer of what group?

6. Who was the oldest singer to have a number one record?

7. What was the name of Mitch Miller's television show?

8. What was Kate Smith's theme song?

9. Mel Tormé came from what city?

10. The Smothers Brothers began their career on whose television show?

The Smothers Brothers.

Quiz #10

TELEVISION THEMES

Match the TV show with its theme song
(Answers on Page 110)

1. *Laverne and Shirley*
2. *The Beverly Hillbillies*
3. *The Jackie Gleason Show*
4. *The Green Hornet*
5. *Your Hit Parade*
6. *Arthur Godfrey's Talent Scouts*
7. *The Sonny and Cher Comedy Hour*
8. *Have Gun Will Travel*
9. *Leave It to Beaver*
10. *The Carol Burnett Show*

a. "Ballad of Jed Clampett"
b. "Flight of the Bumble Bee"
c. "It's Time to Say So Long"
d. "The Beat Goes On"
e. "Be Happy, Go Lucky"
f. "Seems Like Old Times"
g. "Melancholy Serenade"
h. "Ballad of Paladin"
i. "Making our Dreams Come True"
j. "The Toy Parade"

Quiz #11

SONGS

Name the color in the song
(Answers on Page 110)

1. "We All Live in a _____ Submarine"

2. "Song Sung _____, Everybody Knows One"

3. "The _____, _____ Grass of Home"

4. "_____ Sails in the Sunset"

5. "Two _____ Shadows on the Snow"

6. "Beautiful, Beautiful _____ Eyes"

7. "A _____ Sportcoat, and a _____ Carnation"

8. "Out of an _____ Colored Sky"

9. "_____ Haired Daddy of Mine"

10. "Cherry_____ and Apple Blossom _____"

Quiz #12

MUSICAL MOVIES

Who played the star?
(Answers on Page 111)

1. *The Jolson Story*
2. *The Glenn Miller Story*
3. *The Gene Krupa Story*
4. *Funny Girl*
5. *The Benny Goodman Story*
6. *The Great Caruso*
7. *The Joker Is Wild*
8. *With a Song in My Heart*
9. *The Eddie Cantor Story*
10. *The Helen Morgan Story*

FEBRUARY 10¢
NO OTHER LYRIC MAGAZINE CONTAINS THESE EXCLUSIVE SONGS
A SONG LYRICS PUBLICATION
Song Hits
CORRECT LYRICS BY PERMISSION OF COPYRIGHT OWNERS
LATEST POPULAR SONGS of STAGE—SCREEN and RADIO
PRAISE THE LORD AND PASS THE AMMUNITION
THERE WILL NEVER BE ANOTHER YOU
I'M GETTING TIRED SO I CAN SLEEP
I HAD THE CRAZIEST DREAM
THAT OLD BLACK MAGIC
THIS IS THE ARMY, MR. JONES
MOONLIGHT BECOMES YOU
CONSTANTLY
A POEM SET TO MUSIC
SERENADE IN BLUE
WE'RE ALL IN IT
WHEN YOU'RE A LONG, LONG WAY FROM HOME
WHEN MY BLUE MOON TURNS TO GOLD
LIGHT A CANDLE IN THE CHAPEL
MY FLAME WENT OUT LAST NIGHT
THAT SOLDIER OF MINE
I MET HER ON MONDAY
A TOUCH OF TEXAS
I GET THE NECK OF THE CHICKEN
GOBS OF LOVE
LET'S GET LOST
BRAZIL
Dinah Shore
Songs from "HAPPY GO LUCKY"
starring: Dick Powell, Mary Martin, Betty Hutton, Rudy Vallee and others
"DIRECT FROM HOLLYWOOD" – Chico Marx Story
OVER 200 POPULAR HIT SONGS

Dinah Shore

Quiz #13

BROADWAY SHOWS

Match the song with the show
(Answers on Page 111)

1. "Sunrise, Sunset"
2. "Seventy-Six Trombones"
3. "Oh, What A Beautiful Mornin'"
4. "I Got Rhythm"
5. "The Impossible Dream"
6. "Anything You Can Do"
7. "Wilkommen"
8. "You're The Top"
9. "Edelweiss"
10. "Stranger in Paradise"

a. *The Sound of Music*
b. *Cabaret*
c. *Annie Get Your Gun*
d. *The Music Man*
e. *Oklahoma!*
f. *Fiddler on the Roof*
g. *Man of la Mancha*
h. *Three Penny Opera*
i. *Anything Goes*
j. *Girl Crazy*

Quiz #14

SONGS

Richard Rodgers wrote with two lyricists, Lorenz Hart and Oscar Hammerstein. Which one wrote the lyrics to these songs?
(Answers on Page 111)

1. "Edelweiss"

2. "My Funny Valentine"

3. "Getting to Know You"

4. "I Could Write a Book"

5. "There's a Small Hotel"

6. "If I Loved You"

7. "This Nearly Was Mine"

8. "The Most Beautiful Girl in the World"

9. "Bewitched, Bothered, and Bewildered"

10. "Some Enchanted Evening"

Quiz #15

MULTIPLE CHOICE

Singers--what was their biggest hit record
(Answers on Page 112)

1. DON CORNELL
   a) "It Isn't Fair" b) "I'm Yours" c) "I'll Walk Alone"

2. ROY HAMILTON
   a) "Ebb Tide" b) "You'll Never Walk Alone" c) "Yours"

3. TONY MARTIN
   a) "Kiss of Fire" b) "Here" c) "There's No Tomorrow"

4. JULIUS LA ROSA
   a) "Anywhere I Wander" b) "Mobile" c) "Eh Cumpari"

5. KAY STARR
   a) "Side by Side" b) "Wheel of Fortune" c) "Bonaparte's Retreat"

6. MEL TORMÉ
   a) "Careless Hands" b) "The Old Master Painter" c) "Blue Moon"

7. LENA HORNE
   a) "Deed I Do" b) "Stormy Weather" c) "Honey Suckle Rose"

8. BOB MANNING
   a) "The Nearness of You" b) "All I Desire" c) "Venus De Milo"

9. JONI JAMES
   a) "My Love, My Love" b) "Your Cheatin' Heart" c) "Why Don't You Believe Me"

10. JOHNNY MERCER
    a) "Candy" b) "On The Atchison, Topeka, and the Sante Fe" c) "G.I. Jive"

Tony Bennett

Quiz #16

TONY BENNETT
(Answers on Page 112)

1. Who gave Tony Bennett the name Tony Bennett?

2. What name did Tony first use?

3. Name his first number one record?

4. Name his second number one record.

5. Tony co-starred in what movie?

6. How does he sign his paintings?

7. What is Tony's signature song?

8. He did a television show as a summer replacement for what comedian?

9. What was his last top ten record?

10. Who wrote in a *Life* magazine article: "Tony is the Best Singer in the Business"?

Quiz #17

Match the song with the movie
(Answers on Page 112)

1. "The Morning After"
2. "My Kind of Town"
3. "The Windmills of Your Mind"
4. "The Trolley Song"
5. "How Lucky Can You Get"
6. "Thumbelina"
7. "Papa Can You Here Me"
8. "Hold My Hand"
9. "Cheek to Cheek"
10. "A Very Precious Love"

a. *Robin and the Seven Hoods*
b. *Yentl*
c. *The Thomas Crown Affair*
d. *Marjorie Morningstar*
e. *Funny Girl*
f. *Top Hat*
g. *Meet Me in St. Louis*
h. *Hans Christian Anderson*
i. *Susan Slept Here*
j. *The Poseidon Adventure*

Quiz #18

SONGS

Fill in the animal or the bird
(Answers on Page 113)

1. "The _____ Sleeps Tonight"

2. "When the Red, Red _____ Comes Bob-Bob-Bobbin' Along"

3. "Who's Afraid of the Big Bad _____ "

4. "Tie Me _____ down, sport"

5. "The _____ of Happiness"

6. "Cry of the Wild _____ "

7. " _____ in the Tree Top"

8. "Bye, Bye, _____ "

9. "How Much Is That _____ in the Window"

10. "Hold That _____ , Hold That _____ "

Andy Williams

Quiz #19

SINGERS

Name their theme song
(Answers on Page 113)

1. Ted Lewis
2. Judy Garland
3. Al Jolson
4. Sophie Tucker
5. Hildegarde
6. Eddie Cantor
7. Andy Williams
8. Bing Crosby
9. Bobby Vinton
10. Liberace

Quiz #20

NAME THE MARTIN THAT HAD THE HIT RECORD

Is it Dean, Mary, Tony, or Steve
(Answers on Page 113)

1. "Volare"
2. "To Each His Own"
3. "Return to Me"
4. "King Tut"
5. "There's No Tomorrow"
6. "Kiss of Fire"
7. "My Heart Belongs to Daddy"
8. "The Door Is Still Open to My Heart"
9. "Here"
10. "Sway"

Quiz #21

NOVELTY SONGS

Who had the hit?
(Answers on Page 114)

1. "Mr. Custer"
2. "Witch Doctor"
3. "Monster Mash"
4. "Botch-A-Me"
5. "Pepino the Italian Mouse"
6. "Tie Me Kangaroo Down, Sport"
7. "Alvin's Harmonica"
8. "Der Fuehrer's Face"
9. "Na Na, Hey Hey, Kiss Him Goodbye"
10. "Feet Up, Pat Him on the Po-Po"

a. The Chipmunks
b. Bobby Pickett
c. Rolf Harris
d. Rosemary Clooney
e. Lou Monte
f. Guy Mitchell
g. David Seville
h. Larry Verne
i. Spike Jones
j. Steam

Peggy Lee

Al Martino

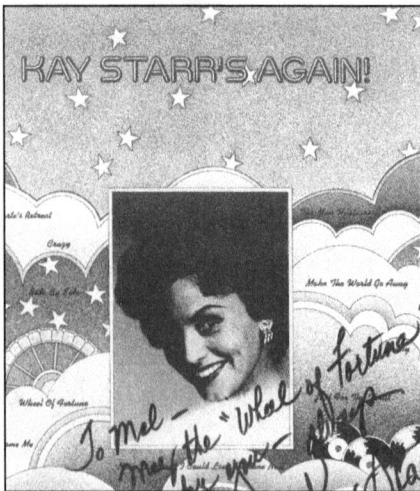

Kay Starr

Quiz #22

GENERAL QUESTIONS
(Answers on Page 114)

1. Peggy Lee became a star singing with what famous band?

2. What female singer has the most #1 singles?

3. Who was Tony Sandler's singing partner?

4. The song "You're So Vain" was written by who?

5. Who was known as "The King of Jazz?"

6. In what year was the long playing vinyl record introduced?

7. Al Martino played singer Johnny Fontane in what movie?

8. What was Judy Garland's real name?

9. Tex Beneke sang and played saxophone with what orchestra?

10. Name the song that was a hit for Kay Starr that also was a hit for Nick Lucas in the 1920s?

Barry Manilow

Quiz #23

BARRY MANILOW
(Answers on Page 114)

1. What is Barry's real name?

2. Where was he born?

3. What was his original musical instrument?

4. He studied music at what school?

5. Played piano at what bath house?

6. He was who's accompanist at the bath house?

7. What did he do for McDonald's and State Farm Insurance?

8. Name his first hit record.

9. Barry recorded what song from the Broadway show *Cats*?

10. What was his biggest selling record?

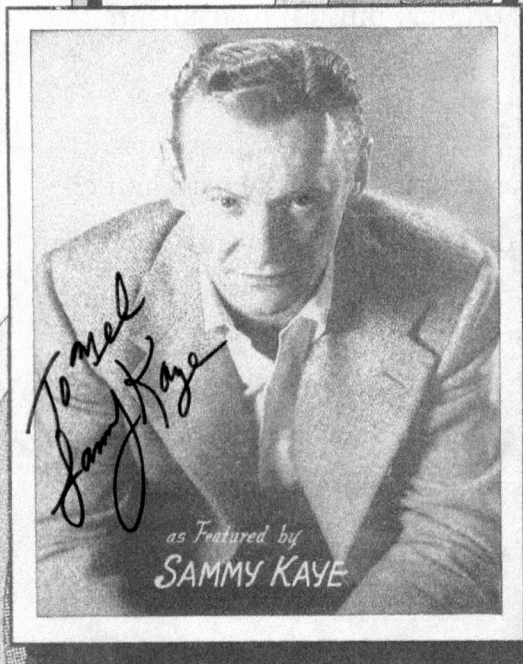

Sammy Kaye

Quiz #24

BIG BANDS - MULTIPLE CHOICE

What was their biggest hit?
(Answers on Page 115)

1. GLENN MILLER
   a) "In the Mood" b) "Moonlight Serenade"
   c) "Tuxedo Junction"

2. HARRY JAMES
   a) "It's Been a Long, Long Time" b) I'll Get By"
   c) "I've Heard That Song Before"

3. JIMMY DORSEY
   a) "Amapola" b) "Green Eyes" c) "Tangerine"

4. SAMMY KAYE
   a) "Harbor Lights" b) "Daddy" c) "Chikery Chick"

5. WOODY HERMAN
   a) "Laura" b) "Caldonia" c) "Blues in the Night"

6. KAY KYSER
   a) "Jingle, Jingle, Jingle" b) "Three Little Fishies"
   c) "Woody Woodpecker"

7. ARTIE SHAW
   a) "Begin the Beguine" b) "Star Dust" c) "Frenesi"

8. TOMMY DORSEY
   a) "I'll Never Smile Again" b) "Dolores" c) "Marie"

9. RUSS MORGAN
   a) "Forever and Ever" b) "So Tired"
   c) "Cruising Down the River"

10. SPIKE JONES
    a) "Chloe" b) "All I Want for Christmas"
    c) "Der Fuehrer's Face"

Harry James

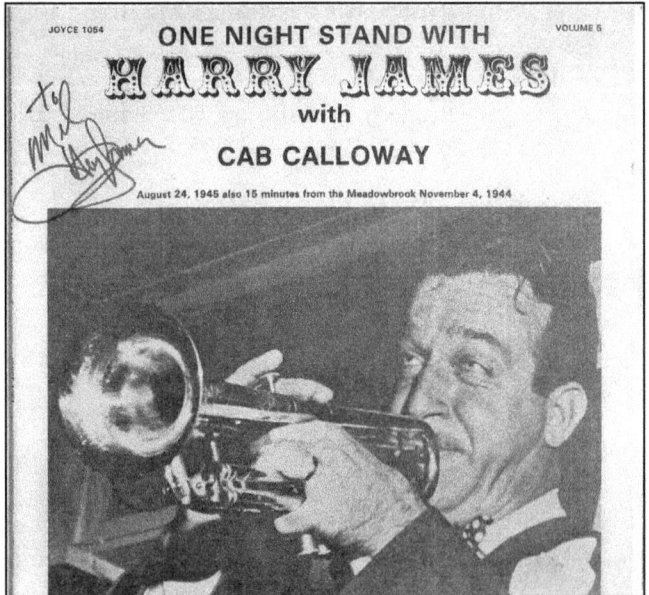

Harry James

Quiz #25

NAMES

Fill in the ladies name
(Answers on Page 115)

1. "I Just Met a Girl Named _____"

2. "All Day, All Night _____"

3. "_____ with the Laughing Face"

4. "Waltzing _____, Waltzing
   _____"

5. "_____, There's a Minister Handy"

6. "Every Star Above, Knows the One I Love, Sweet
   _____"

7. "_____, Oh, _____, Say
   Have You Seen _____"

8. "In My Sweet Little _____ Blue
   Gown"

9. "_____ O' My Heart, I Love You"

10. "After All Is Said and Done, There Is Really Only
    One, _____, _____ it's
    You"

Quiz #26

NICKNAMES

Match the singers with their nicknames
(Answers on Page 115)

1. Louis Armstrong
2. Bing Crosby
3. Patti Page
4. Frank Sinatra
5. Jimmy Durante
6. Georgia Gibbs
7. Mel Tormé
8. Eddie Cantor
9. Sophie Tucker
10. Arthur Tracy

a. The Voice
b. The Velvet Fog
c. The Singing Rage
d. The Groaner
e. Last of the red hot mamas
f. Her Nibbs
g. Satchmo
h. Schnozzola
i. The Street Singer
j. Banjo Eyes

Quiz #27

ONE HIT WONDERS

Match the vocal group with their only hit record
(Answers on Page 116)

1. "Walk Right In"
2. "Puttin' on the Ritz"
3. "It's Almost Tomorrow"
4. "Our Day Will Come"
5. "Winchester Cathedral"
6. "Happy, Happy Birthday Baby"
7. "Graduation Day"
8. "No More"
9. "Baubles, Bangles, and Beads"
10. "I'd Like to Teach the World to Sing"

a. Ruby and the Romantics
b. The Tune Weavers
c. The Dream Weavers
d. The Rover Boys
e. Taco
f. The Rooftop Singers
g. Kirby Stone Four
h. The Hillside Singers
i. New Vaudeville Band
j. The DeJohn Sisters

The Andrew Sisters

The McGuire Sisters

Quiz #28

TWO GREAT SISTER VOCAL GROUPS
The Andrews Sisters and The McGuire Sisters

Which group had the hit record?
(Answers on Page 116)

1. "Something's Gotta Give"

2. "May You Always"

3. "Rum and Coca-Cola"

4. "I Can Dream, Can't I?"

5. "Muskrat Ramble"

6. "Don't Sit Under the Apple Tree"

7. "He"

8. "Shoo-Shoo Baby"

9. "Sincerely"

10. "Bei Mir Bist Du Schoen"

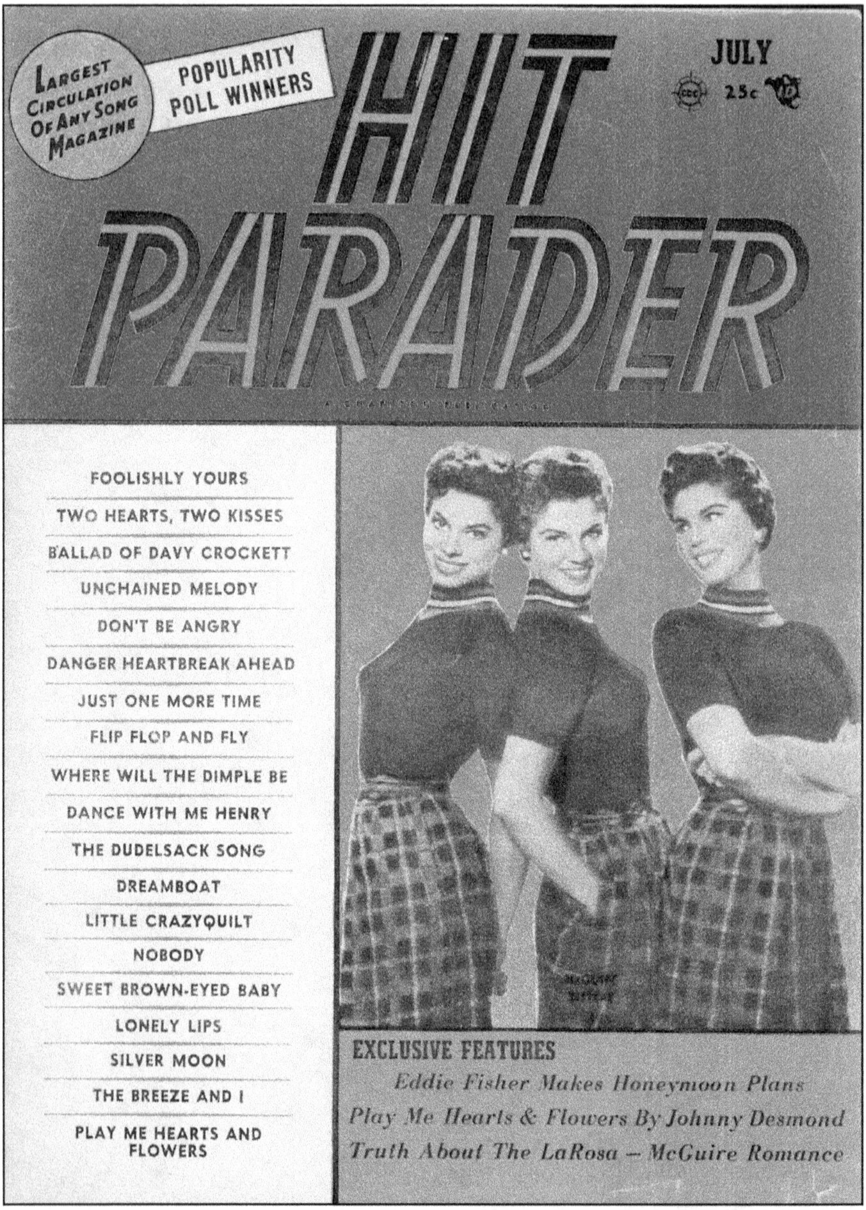

The McGuire Sisters

Quiz #29

NAME THE BODY PART IN THE SONG
(Answers on Page 116)

1. Those _____ in Your Hair

2. Around Her _____ She Wore a Yellow Ribbon

3. Picture You, Upon My _____, Just Tea for Two, and Two for Tea

4. Your _____ Are The _____ of a Woman In Love

5. With These _____, I Will Cling to You

6. You've Gotta Have _____, All You Really Need Is _____

7. Turned Up Hose, Turned Down _____

8. All I Want for Christmas Is My Two Front _____

9. _____ belina, _____ belina, Tiny Little Thing

10. She's Got Rings on Her _____, and Bells on Her _____

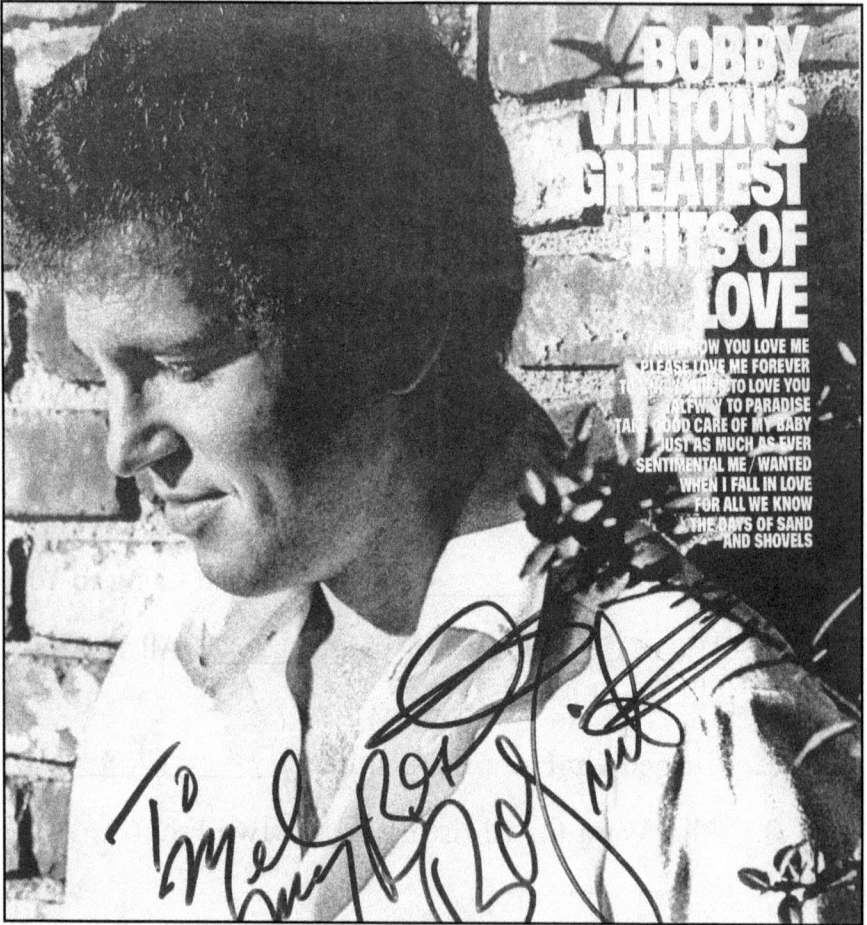

Bobby Vinton

Quiz #30

GENERAL QUESTIONS
(Answers on Page 117)

1. What was Bobby Vinton's 1st hit record?

2. Name the singer who was known for wearing white bucs?

3. Harry James was married to what famous movie star?

4. In what year were the Grammy Awards introduced?

5. Teresa Brewer's 1st record became a #1 record. Name the song.

6. Name the singer who was the second runner up to Miss America in 1965.

7. Who had the "Band of Renown?"

8. Name the four Lennon Sisters.

9. What was Sammy Kaye's famous catch phrase?

10. What instrument did Vaughn Monroe play?

'LL ALWAYS BE WITH YOU
To Mel
All my Best
Les Brown
WORDS AND MUSIC
BY
MARJORIE GOETSCHIUS
AND
EDNA OSSER
Introduced by
LES BROWN
MANNING
BROADWAY MUSIC CORPORA

Les Brown

Quiz #31

SINGING COMMERCIALS

Fill in the product
(Answers on Page 117)

1. You deserve a break today. So get up and get away to,
   _____ .

2. Call _____ _____ , that's the
   name, and away go troubles down the drain.

3. When you're out of _____ , you're out of
   beer

4. Oh, I wish I were an _____ _____
   Wiener. That is what I'd truly like to be.

5. Charlie says, love my _____ ___
   _____ , don't know any other candy that I
   love so well.

6. Like a good neighbor, _____
   _____ is There.

7. I love _____ , it's rich and chocolaty.
   Mama puts it in my milk for extra energy.

8. You can take _____ out of the
   country, but, you can't take the country out of
   _____ .

9. Use _____ Blue Blades for the quickest,
   slickest shaves of all.

10. Have you tried _____ . The best breakfast
    food in the Land.

Quiz #32

INTRUMENTAL HITS

Who had the hit record
(Answers on Page 117)

1. "Autumn Leaves"
2. "Love Is Blue"
3. "Cherry Pink and Apple Blossom White"
4. "Melody of Love"
5. "Dragnet"
6. "Lisbon Antiqua"
7. "Oh"
8, "Poor People of Paris"
9. "Exodus"
10. "Walk Don't Run"

a. Ferrante and Teicher
b. Perez Prado
c. Ray Anthony
d. Nelson Riddle
e. Pee Wee Hunt
f. The Ventures
g. Paul Mauriat
h. Roger Williams
i. Les Baxter
j. Billy Vaughn

Quiz #33

THE DORSEY BROTHERS

Is it Tommy or Jimmy?

(Answers on Page 118)

1. Who had the most hit records?

2. Bob Eberly and Helen O'Connel sang with whom?

3. Which brother is older?

4. Dick Haymes sang with which band?

5. Who was known as "The Sentimental Gentleman of Swing"?

6. Kitty Kallen sang with what band?

7. Who had the hit record "So Rare"?

8. Sy Oliver was the jazz arranger for whom?

9. Connie Haines sang with whom?

10. Which brother recorded for Decca Records?

Barbra Streisand

Quiz #34

BARBRA STREISSAND

(Answers on Page 118)

1. What is Barbra's middle name?

2. Name the nightclub that she first appeared in.

3. What was her first Broadway show?

4. The male star of the show became her first husband. What was his name?

5. Name the first major Broadway show that she starred in?

6. This show was based on the life of what famous entertainer?

7. What was her first hit record?

8. Name her first album?

9. She directed and starred in what move, where she played a Jewish boy. What was it?

10. Barbra had a number one record, "You Don't Bring Me Flowers." Who sang a duet with her?

Mitch Miller

Quiz #35

TELEVISION THEMES

Match the TV show with its theme song
(Answers on Page 118)

1. *The Jeffersons*
2. *The Jack Benny Program*
3. *Cheers*
4. *You Bet Your Life*
5. *The Andy Griffith Show*
6. *Sing Along With Mitch*
7. *American Bandstand*
8. *Gunsmoke*
9. *The Mary Tyler Moore Show*
10. *The Gene Autry Show*

a. "Where Everybody Knows Your Name"
b. "The Fishin' Hole"
c. "Hooray for Captain Spaulding"
d. "Let Me Hear a Melody"
e. "Movin' On Up"
f. "I'm Back in the Saddle Again"
g. "Love in Bloom"
h. "Bandstand Boogie"
i. "Love Is All Around"
j. "Old Trail"

Patti Page

Quiz #36

PATTI PAGE
(Answers on Page 119)

1. Where was Patti born?

2. What is her real name?

3. Most of Patti's hit records were on what record label?

4. Name her first number one record.

5. Patti shared what hit song with Les Paul and Mary Ford?

6. What was her biggest selling record?

7. Name her second biggest selling record?

8. What was Patti's theme song on her television show?

9. Patti briefly sang with what famous band leader?

10. Her last hit was the theme of a movie. Name the song.

Quiz #37

CITIES, STATES, AND COUNTRIES

Name The Place
(Answers on Page 119)

1. Back Home Again, in _____

2. I Left My Heart in, _____ _____

3. I Found My Love in _____

4. You're Sure to Fall in Love with Old
   _____

5. It's A Treat To Beat Your Feet on the
   _____ Mud

6. Meet Me in _____ _____,
   _____

7. _____ Must Be Heaven, for My
   Mother Came from There

8. I Want to Be a Part of It _____ _____,
   _____ _____

9. I Was Dancing with My Darlin' to the
   _____ Waltz

10. Nothing Could Be Finer than to Be in
    _____, in the Morning

Quiz #38

FILL IN THE LADIES NAME
(Answers on Page 119)

1. Wait Till the Sunshine's _____

2. If You Knew _____, Like I knew
   _____

3. Goodnight _____, Goodnight
   _____ I'll See You in My Dreams

4. Once in Love With _____, Always in
   Love with _____

5. Hey, _____, I'm Gonna Marry You

6. Hello _____, Well, Hello
   _____, It's So Nice to Have You Back
   Where You Belong

7. _____, Sweet as Apple Cider

8. After All Is Said and Done, There Is Really Only One.
   Oh, Oh, _____, _____, it's
   you

9. When I Go to Sleep, I Never count Sheep. I count
   all the Charms about _____

10. For It Was _____,
    _____, Proud as Any Name Can Be

Penny Arcade cards
Kitty Kallen, Pat Boone
Nat "King" Cole, Teresa Brewer

Quiz #39

VOCAL GROUPS

What group had these hit records?
(Answers on Page 120)

1. "Moments to Remember"
2. "Mr. Sandman"
3. "Leaving on a Jet Plane"
4. "It's a Blue World"
5. "P.S. I Love You"
6. "Monday, Monday"
7. "Rag Mop"
8. "Little Darlin'"
9. "The Little Shoemaker"
10. "Charlie on the M.T.A."

a. The Kingston Trio
b. The Mamas and The Papas
c. The Diamonds
d. The Chordettes
e. The Four Lads
f. The Ames Brothers
g. Peter, Paul, and Mary
h. The Gaylords
i. The Hilltoppers
j. The Four Freshmen

Margaret Whiting

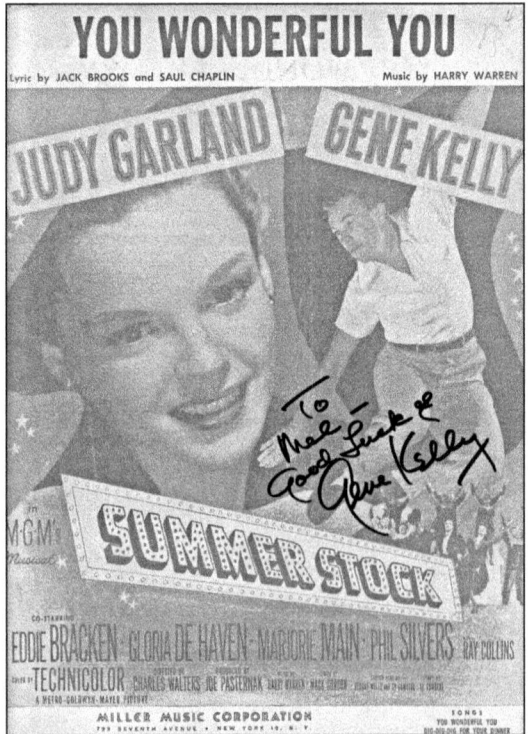

Judy Garland and Gene Kelly

Quiz #40

GENERAL QUESTIONS
(Answers on Page 120)

1. Bobby Darin began his career as a musician. What instrument did he play?

2. Who was the first act to appear on *American Bandstand*?

3. What Country singer has sold the most records in history?

4. Margaret Whitting's father was a famous song writer. What was his name?

5. What was the name of Arlo Guthrie's father?

6. Don Cornell sang with what band?

7. Name the singer/actress who starred in the movie *The Singing Nun*?

8. Bob Flanigan was the lead singer for what vocal group?

9. The song, "I'd Like to Teach the World to Sing" became a commercial for what product?

10. What song did Gene Kelly sing in the movie *Marjorie Morningstar*?

Quiz #41

NAME THE FOOD OR DRINK
(Answers on Page 120)

1. Mary Had a Little _____

2. I'm in Love with You, _____

3. _____ Tree, Very Pretty

4. She Had Kisses Sweeter than _____

5. Don't Sit Under the _____ Tree

6. You're the _____ in My
   _____

7. Cool, Clear, _____

8. When My _____ Walks Down the
   Street

9. The Night They Invented _____

10. Life Is Just a Bowl of _____

Quiz #42

TELEVISION THEMES

Match the TV Show with its theme song
(Answers on Page 121)

1. *The Golden Girls*
2. *Touched by an Angel*
3. *Coke Time with Eddie Fisher*
4. *Designing Women*
5. *The Red Skelton Show*
6. *Alfred Hitchcock Presents*
7. *I've Got a Secret*
8. *The Perry Como Show*
9. *The George Burns and Gracie Allen Show*
10. *The Goldbergs*

a. "Toselli Serenade"
b. "May I Sing to You"
c. "Thank You for Being a Friend"
d. "Plink, Plank, Plunk"
e. "Love Nest"
f. "Funeral March of a Marionette"
g. "Georgia on my Mind"
h. "Dream Along with Me"
i. "Holiday for Strings"
j. "Walk with You"

Teresa Brewer

Quiz #43

MULTIPLE CHOICE

Singers – what was their biggest hit record
(Answers on Page 121)

1. THERESA BREWER
   a) "Ricochet" b) "Jilted" c) "Music-Music-Music"

2. DINAH SHORE
   a) "Buttons and Bows" b) "Sweet Violets" c) "Candy"

3. AL MARTINO
   a) "Here in My Heart" b) "Spanish Eyes"
   c) "I Love You Because"

4. VAUGHN MONROE
   a) "Ballerina" b) "Ghost Riders in the Sky"
   c) "There, I've Said It Again"

5. VERA LYNN
   a) "Yours" b) "Auf Wiedersehen" c) "You Can't Be True Dear"

6. MARIO LANZA
   a) "The Loveliest Night of the Year"
   b) "Because You're Mine" c) "Be My Love"

7. GEORGIA GIBBS
   a) "Kiss of Fire" b) "Seven Lonely Days"
   c) "My Favorite Song"

8. DENNIS DAY
   a) "Clancy Lowered the Boom" b) "Mam'selle"
   c) "Dear Hearts and Gentle People"

9. JO STAFFORD
   a) "You Belong to Me" b) "Shrimp Boats"
   c) "Make Love to Me"

10. GUY MITCHELL
    a) "The Roving Kind" b) "Pittsburgh Pennsylvania"
    c) "My Heart Cries for You"

Dennis Day

Quiz #44

SONGS

Fill in the weather or the season
(Answers on Page 121)

1. The _____ leaves, drift by my window

2. Walkin' in a _____ Wonderland

3. _____ drops Keep Fallin' on My Head

4. Let It _____, Let it _____, Let it _____

5. When It's _____ Time in the Rockies

6. You Are My _____

7. A _____ Day, in London Town

8. _____ Weather

9. April _____

10. Roll Out Those Lazy, _____, crazy days of _____

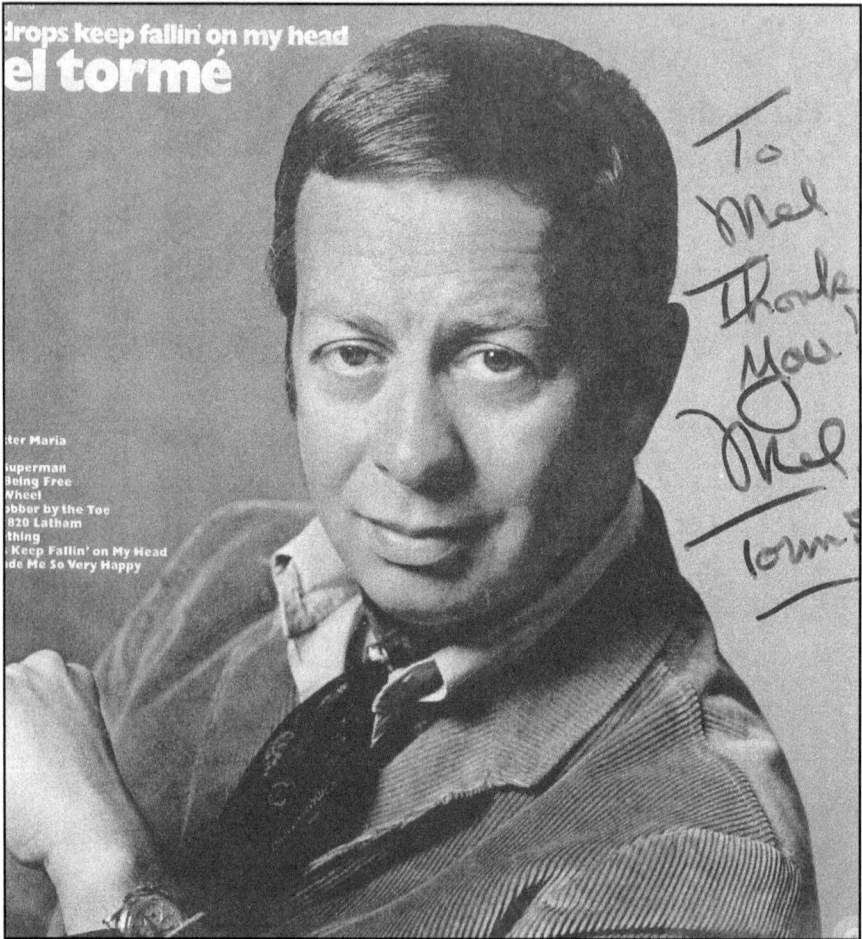

Mel Tormé

Quiz #45

MEL TORMÉ
(Answers on Page 122)

1. Mel started singing professionally at what age?

2. As a youngster, he appeared on what kid's radio program?

3. As a teenager, he played drums and sang with what big band?

4. Name his backup vocal group.

5. What was Mel's nickname?

6. Name the well known Christmas song that he wrote.

7. Who had the hit record of this song?

8. What was the title of his autobiography?

9. Mel became a regular as a singer and musical advisor on what singer's television show?

10. In the 1980s, he became a regular on what television sitcom?

Quiz #46

CITIES, STATES, AND COUNTRIES

Name the place
(Answers on Page 122)

1. I Love _____ in the Winter

2. Deep in the Heart of _____

3. The Windy City, _____ Is

4. _____ Here I Come

5. There's a Pawn Shop on the Corner In _____, _____

6. From _____, With Love

7. Why Did I Ever Leave _____

8. Stars Fell on _____, Last Night

9. _____ Town, My _____ Town

10. Moonlight in _____

Quiz #47

BROADWAY SHOWS

Match the song with the show
(Answers on Page 122)

1. "Getting to Know You"
2. "Tonight"
3. "Hey Look Me Over"
4. "Razzle Dazzle"
5. "I Could Have Danced all Night"
6. "Love Look Away"
7. "Heart"
8. "Tea for Two"
9. "Standing on the Corner"
10. "One"

a. *The King and I*
b. *Wildcat*
c. *The Most Happy Fella*
d. *A Chorus Line*
e. *No, No, Nanette*
f. *My Fair Lady*
g. *Chicago*
h. *West Side Story*
i. *Flower Drum Song*
j. *Damn Yankees*

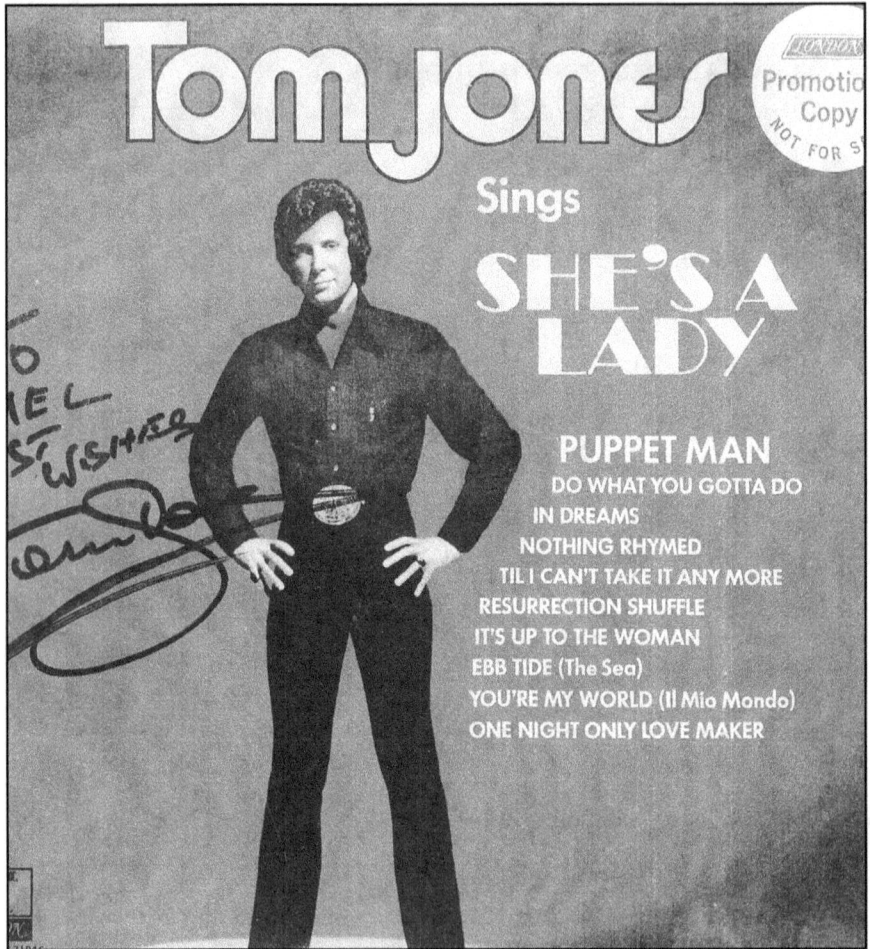

Tom Jones

Quiz #48

ENGELBERT HUMPERDINCK OR TOM JONES

Who had the hit record?
(Answers on Page 123)

1. "What's New, Pussycat?"

2. "Release Me"

3. "The Last Waltz"

4. "It's Not Unusual"

5. "After the Lovin'"

6. "Green, Green Grass of Home"

7. "Thunderball"

8. "Winter World of Love"

9. "Delilah"

10. "A Man Without Love"

Engelbert Humperdinck

Quiz #49

NAME THE BODY PART IN THE SONG
(Answers on Page 123)

1. I Left My _____ in San Francisco

2. You've Got the Cutest Little Baby _____

3. _____ of My _____, I Love that Melody

4. When Your_____ Has Turned to Silver

5. Two Left _____, But, Oh So Neat, Has Sweet Georgia Brown

6. I've Got You Under My _____

7. When Irish _____ Are Smiling

8. Put Your _____ Around Me Honey, Hold Me Tight

9. A Bushel and a Peck, and a Hug Around The _____

10. Put Your _____ on My _____

Frankie Laine

Julius La Rosa

Quiz #50

GENERAL QUESTIONS
(Answers on Page 123)

1. "Thanks for the Memory" was whose theme song?

2. What did Les Paul invent?

3. What were the first names of The Carpenters?

4. Name the television host who fired Julius La Rosa on the air.

5. Name the #1 record that Johnny Mathis had, singing duet with Denise Williams.

6. Dorothy Collins sang on what television show?

7. Who was Lawrence Welk's first Champagne lady?

8. Who was known as "The Street Singer"?

9. Chevrolet sponsored what singer on television?

10. Who was the lead singer of "The Ink Spots"?

Johnny Mathis

Quiz #51

BROADWAY SHOWS

Match the song with the show
(Answers on Page 124)

1. "Hey There"
2. "I Am What I Am"
3. "Some Enchanted Evening"
4. "Bosom Buddies"
5. "Thank Heaven for Little Girls"
6. "Shalom"
7. "Let Me Entertain You"
8. "A Bushel And a Peck"
9. "Memory"
10. "If I Loved You"

a. *Gigi*
b. *Mame*
c. *Milk and Honey*
d. *Cats*
e. *Le Cage aux Folles*
f. *The Pajama Game*
g. *Guys and Dolls*
h. *South Pacific*
i. *Gypsy*
j. *Carousel*

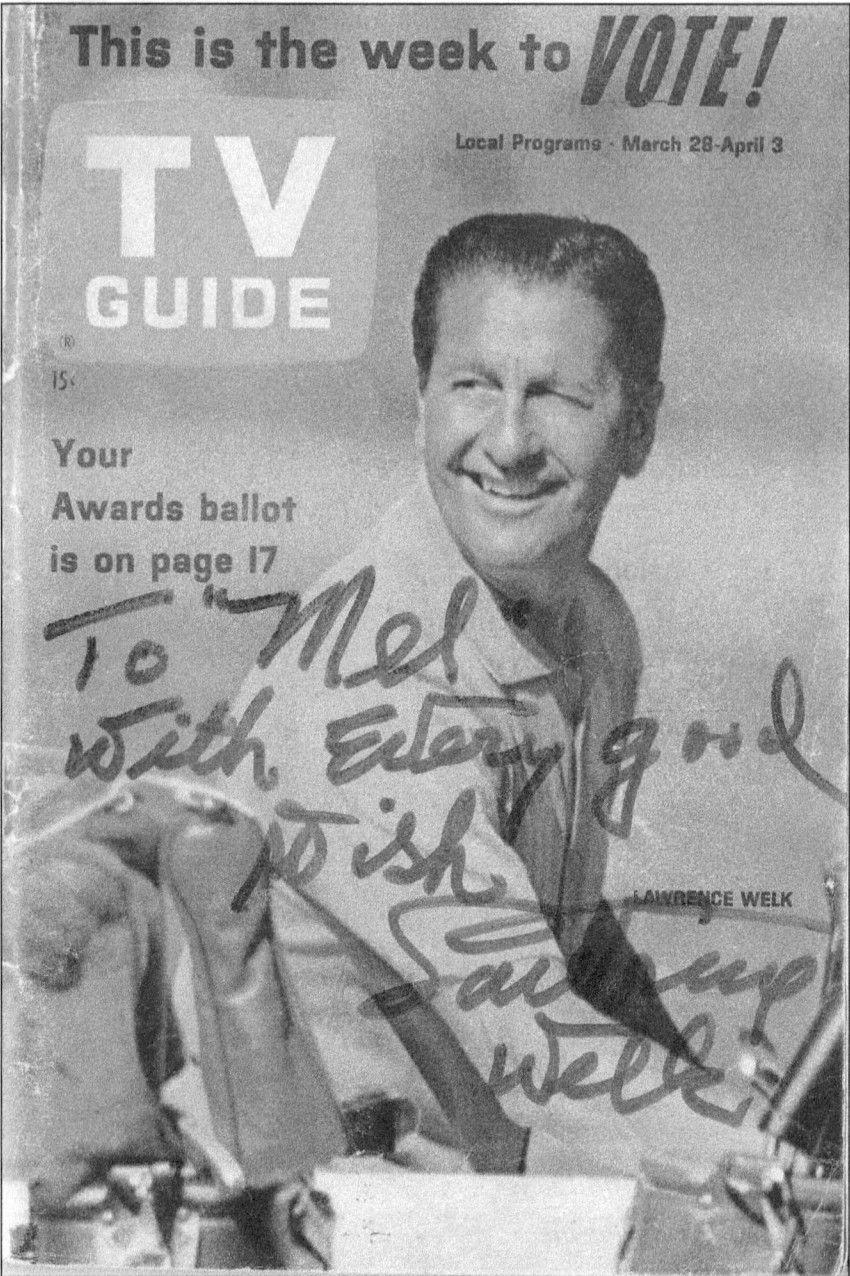

Lawrence Welk

Quiz #52

SONGS

Fill in the man's name
(Answers on Page 124)

1. What's It All About, _____

2. I'm Just Wild About _____

3. I'm _____, the Sailor Man

4. _____, You Made the Pants Too Long

5. _____ Row, the Boat Ashore

6. Because He's Just My _____

7. _____, My Boy, Oh, _____, My Boy

8. _____ _____, King of the Wild Frontier

9. Ode To _____ _____

10. _____, Oo - Oo - Oo - Oo - Oo - Oo -, _____, My Love

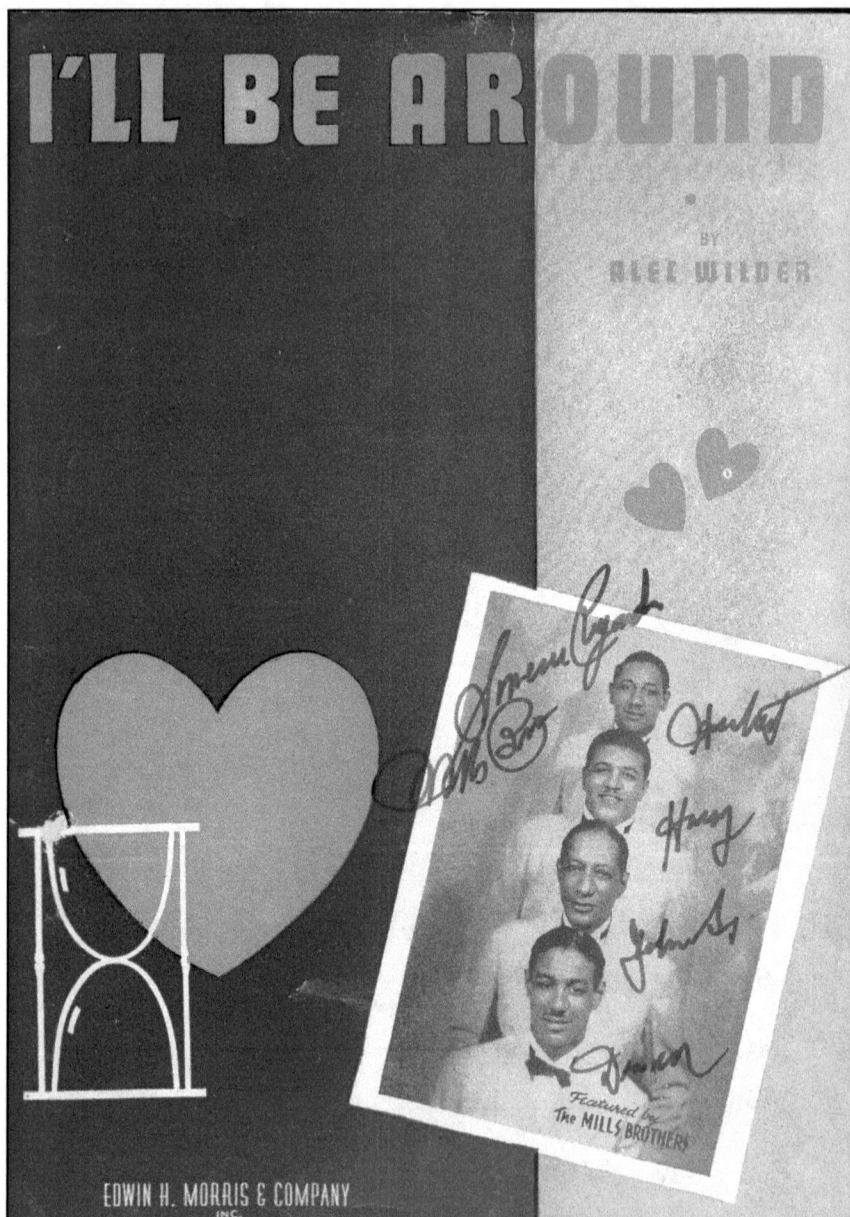

The Mills Brothers

Quiz #53

TWO GREAT VOCAL GROUPS

The Ink Spots or The Mills Brothers?
(Answers on Page 124)

1. Who had the hit record "Till Then"?

2. Who had the hit record "We Three"?

3. Who had the hit record "If I Didn't Care"?

4. A father & son sang with which group?

5. Who had the hit record "Daddy's Little Girl"?

6. Who had the hit record "To Each His Own"?

7. Two brothers sang with which group?

8. Who had the hit record "I Don't Want To Set The World On Fire"?

9. Who had the hit record "The Glow-Worm"?

10. Which group was known for doing imitations of musical instruments?

Quiz #54

ONE HIT WONDERS

Match the singers with their only hit record
(Answers on Page 125)

1. "Harper Valley, P.T.A."
2. "Feelings"
3. "Rose Garden"
4. "The Last Farewell"
5. "Yesterday, When I Was Young"
6. "Volare"
7. "Ivory Tower"
8. "I Remember You"
9. "Cinco Robles"
10. "The City of New Orleans"

a. Roger Whittaker
b. Roy Clark
c. Arlo Guthrie
d. Jeannie C. Riley
e. Domenico Modugno
f. Lynn Anderson
g. Morris Albert
h. Russell Arms
i. Frank Ifield
j. Cathy Carr

Quiz #55

MATCH THE SONG WITH THE MOVIE
(Answers on Page 125)

1. "That's Amore"
2. "Count Your Blessings"
3. "Thanks for the Memory"
4. "I Just Called to Say I Love You"
5. "Be Our Guest"
6. "I Can't Begin to Tell You"
7. "More"
8. "Boogie Woogie Bugle Boy"
9. "Jean"
10. "Something's Gotta Give"

a. *Beauty and the Beast*
b. *Mondo Cane*
c. *The Caddy*
d. *The Prime of Miss Jean Brodie*
e. *Big Broadcast of 1938*
f. *Daddy Long Legs*
g. *Buck Privates*
h. *The Dolly Sisters*
i. *The Woman in Red*
j. *White Christmas*

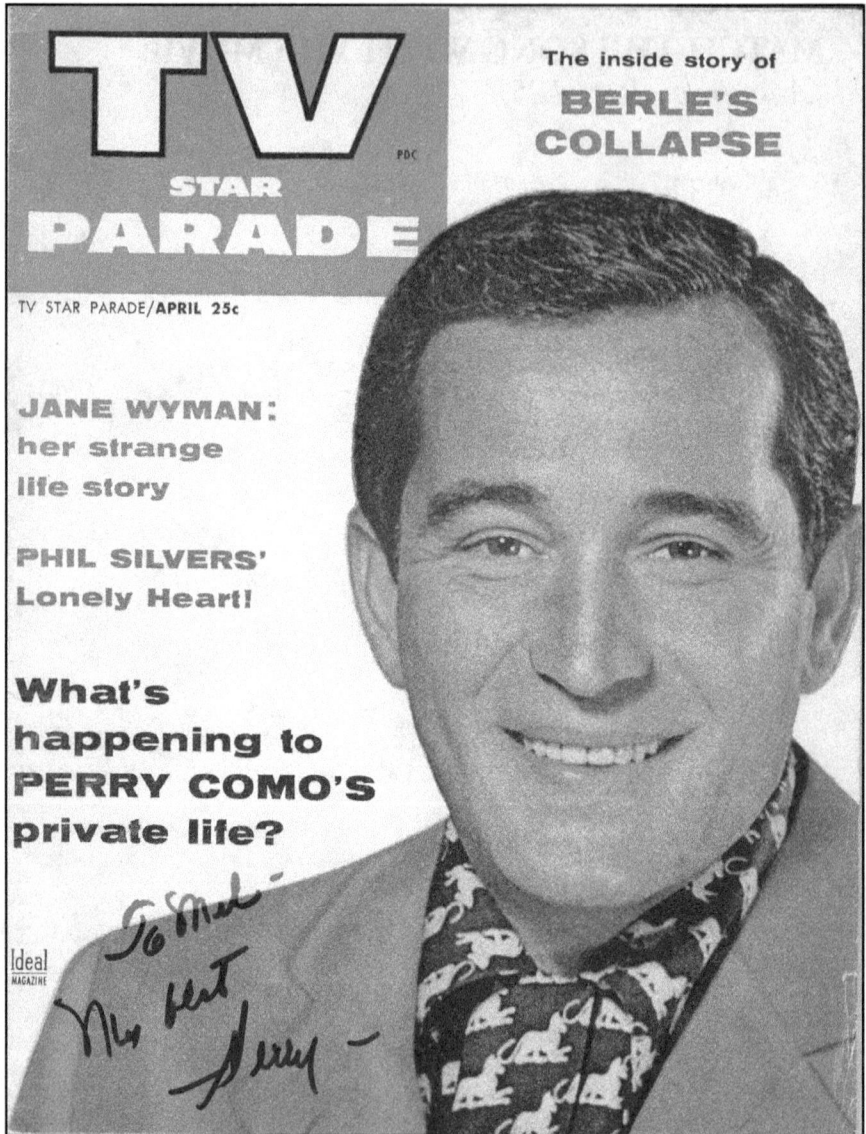

Perry Como

Quiz #56

PERRY COMO
(Answers on Page 125)

1. Before he became a singer, what did Perry do for a living?

2. Perry was the vocalist with what band?

3. Perry appeared on *The Chesterfield Show* on CBS Radio. Who was his co-star?

4. He recorded for the same record company for over 50 years. Name the company?

5. What was Perry's first hit record?

6. Perry often sang with what female vocal group?

7. He sang a duet with what singer on the song "Maybe"?

8. On his television show, what was his theme song?

9. What was Perry's last hit record?

10. What was Perry's last number one record?

Vic Damone

Quiz #57

GENERAL QUESTIONS
(Answers on Page 126)

1. Name the record that Vic Damone had from the Broadway musical: *My Fair Lady*

2. What are the first names of Simon and Garfunkle?

3. Name Guy Lombardo's brother, who wrote many of the band's hit songs.

4. What band did Bob Eberly sing with?

5. What band did Ray Eberly sing with?

6. What is the most popular sports related song?

7. Andy Williams has a theater in Branson, Missouri. Name the Theater.

8. Dave Guard sang with what vocal group?

9. What was Helen Reddy's biggest selling record?

10. Paul Anka wrote the theme song for what television show?

Paul Anka

Quiz #58

ONE HIT WONDERS

Match the vocal group with their only hit record
(Answers on Page 126)

1. "The Unicorn"
2. "Born Too Late"
3. "Chanson D'Amour"
4. "Teach Me Tonight"
5. "Green Fields"
6. "Tonight You Belong to Me"
7. "Flowers on the Wall"
8. "Earth Angel"
9. "It's a Sin to Tell a Lie"
10. "Michael Row the Boat Ashore"

a. The Poni Tails
b. The Statler Brothers
c. Art and Dotty Todd
d. The Brothers Four
e. The Irish Rovers
f. Patience and Prudence
g. The Penquins
h. The DeCastro Sisters
i. The Highwaymen
j. Somethin' Smith and The Redheads

Guy Lombardo

Quiz #59

SONGS

Name the color in the song
(Answers on Page 126)

1. Put On Your Old _____ Bonnet

2. _____ Tambourine

3. Tie A _____ Ribbon Round The Old Oak Tree

4. _____ Panther Theme

5. _____ Roses For A _____ Lady

6. Sweet _____, Sweeter Thank The Roses

7. I'm Dreaming Of A _____ Christmas

8. _____ Tree, Very Pretty

9. Won't It Make My _____ Eyes _____

10. A-Tisket, A-Tasket, A _____ And _____ Basket

Nat King Cole

Quiz #60

CHRISTMAS SONGS

Match the singer with their Christmas Song
(Answers on Page 127)

1. "Rockin' Around the Christmas Tree"
2. "It's A Holly Jolly Christmas"
3. "Do You Hear What I Hear?"
4. "Home for the Holidays"
5. "The Christmas Song"
6. "Have Yourself a Merry Little Christmas"
7. "Feliz Navidad"
8. "I Saw Mommy Kissing Santa Claus"
9. "Blue Christmas"
10. "Jingle Bell Rock"

a. Elvis Presley
b. Perry Como
c. Brenda Lee
d. Bobby Helms
e. Judy Garland
f. Jose Feliciano
g. Burl Ives
h. Jimmy Boyd
i. Bing Crosby
j. Nat King Cole

Dean Martin

Quiz #61

DEAN MARTIN
(Answers on Page 127)

1. Before becoming a singer, what sport did Dean Martin participate in ?

2. He first did an act with Jerry Lewis at what Atlantic City night club?

3. Name Dean and Jerry's first movie.

4. Dean and Jerry became monthly regulars on what television show?

5. What hit record did Dean have from the move *The Caddy*?

6. In what year did Dean and Jerry break up?

7. Name Dean's biggest selling record.

8. What was his theme song on television?

9. Dean did a series of movies, in which he played a comic James Bond character. Name the character that he played.

10. Name Dean's fellow members of The Rat Pack.

Gale Storm

Quiz #62

TWO GREAT VOCAL GROUPS

The Modernaires or The Pied Pipers
(Answers on Page 127)

1. Who had the hit record "Kalamazoo"?

2. Tommy Dorsey featured which group?

3. Who had the hit record "Dream"?

4. Marion Hutton sang with which group?

5. "Stardust" was a hit record for which group?

6. Paula Kelly sand with which group?

7. "My Happiness" was a hit for which group?

8. Jo Stafford sang with which group?

9. Tex Beneke often sang duets with which group?

10. Who had the hit record "Juke Box Saturday Night"?

Quiz #63

TELEVISION THEMES

Match the TV Show with its theme song
(Answers on Page 128)

1. *All in the Family*
2. *The Lone Ranger*
3. *Friends*
4. *The Lawrence Welk Show*
5. *The Roy Rogers Show*
6. *Happy Days*
7. *Make Room for Daddy*
8. *The Partridge Family*
9. *Baretta*
10. *Medic*

a. "Rock Around the Clock"
b. "Blue Star"
c. "Happy Trails"
d. "Keep Your Eye on the Sparrow"
e. "Those Were The Days"
f. "Come On Get Happy"
g. "Bubbles In the Wine"
h. "William Tell Overture"
i. "I'll Be There for You"
j. "Danny Boy"

ANSWERS

QUIZ #1 *(from page 3)*

1. The Copacabana
2. Grossingers
3. Eddie Cantor
4. Coke Time
5. Debbie Reynolds, Elizabeth Taylor, Connie Stevens
6. RCA Victor
7. "Thinking of You"
8. "Wish You Were Here"
9. "Oh, My Pa-Pa"
10. "Count Your Blessings"

QUIZ #2 *(from page 5)*

1. d
2. f
3. g
4. c
5. b
6. i
7. h
8. e
9. a
10. j

QUIZ #3   *(from page 7)*

1. Dick Clark
2. Benny Goodman
3. "Secret Love"
4. Accordion
5. The Platters
6. Ed, Gene, Joe, Vic
7. George Gershwin
8. "God Bless America"
9. *The Graduate*
10. Jerry Moss

QUIZ #4   *(from page 9)*

1. 3
2. 16
3. 76
4. 8
5. 6
6. 2
7. 10
8. 10
9. 5
10. 1

QUIZ #5   *(from page 11)*

1. b
2. f
3. h
4. a
5. g
6. j
7. c
8. i
9. d
10. e

QUIZ #6   *(from page 13)*
1. Armour
2. Cracker Jacks
3. Alka Seltzer
4. Doublemint
5. Texaco
6. Almond Joy - Mounds
7. Pepsi
8. Chock Full O' Nuts
9. Rice-A-Roni
10. Pillsbury

QUIZ #7   *(from page 15)*
1. Tony Pastor
2. Betty
3. Mitch Miller
4. "You're Just in Love"
5. "Come on – a My House"
6. "Hey There" and "This Old House"
7. "Mambo Italiano"
8. Bing Crosby
9. Debby Boone
10. *White Christmas*

QUIZ #8   *(from page 17)*
1. Benny Goodman
2. Benny Goodman
3. Artie Shaw
4. Artie Shaw
5. Artie Shaw
6. Benny Goodman
7. Benny Goodman
8. Benny Goodman
9. Artie Shaw
10. Artie Shaw

QUIZ #9   *(from page 19)*

1. David Seville
2. Freddy Martin
3. "The Candy Man"
4. *Rawhide*
5. The Four Aces
6. Louis Armstrong ("Hello, Dolly")
7. *Sing-A-Long With Mitch*
8. "When the Moon Comes over the Mountain"
9. Chicago
10. *The Tonight Show* Starring Jack Paar

QUIZ #10   *(from page 21)*

1. i
2. a
3. g
4. b
5. e
6. f
7. d
8. h
9. j
10. c

QUIZ #11   *(from page 22)*

1. Yellow
2. Blue
3. Green - Green
4. Red
5. Purple
6. Brown
7. White-Pink
8. Orange
9. Silver
10. Pink-White

QUIZ #12 *(from page 23)*
1. Larry Parks
2. James Stewart
3. Sal Mineo
4. Barbra Streisand
5. Steve Allen
6. Mario Lanza
7. Frank Sinatra
8. Susan Hayward
9. Keefe Brasselle
10. Polly Bergen

QUIZ #13 *(from page 25)*
1. f
2. d
3. e
4. j
5. g
6. c
7. b
8. i
9. a
10. h

QUIZ #14 *(from page 26)*
1. Oscar Hammerstein
2. Lorenz Hart
3. Oscar Hammerstein
4. Lorenz Hart
5. Lorenz Hart
6. Oscar Hammerstein
7. Oscar Hammerstein
8. Lorenz Hart
9. Lorenz Hart
10. Oscar Hammerstein

QUIZ #15   *(from page 27)*

1. a
2. b
3. c
4. c
5. b
6. a
7. b
8. a
9. c
10 .b

QUIZ #16   *(from page 29)*

1. Bob Hope
2. Joe Bari
3. "Because of You"
4. "Cold, Cold Heart"
5. The Oscar
6. Anthony Benedetto [his real name]
7. "I Left My Heart in San Francisco "
8. Jackie Gleason
9. "In the Middle of an Island"
10. Frank Sinatra

QUIZ #17   *(from page 30)*

1. j
2. a
3. c
4. g
5. e
6. h
7. b
8. i
9. f
10. d

QUIZ #18 *(from page 31)*
1. Lion
2. Robin
3. Wolf
4. Kangaroo
5. Bluebird
6. Goose
7. Sparrow
8. Blackbird
9. Doggie
10. Tiger-Tiger

QUIZ #19 *(from page 33)*
1. "Me and My Shadow"
2. "Over the Rainbow"
3. "April Showers"
4. "Some of These Days"
5. "Darling, Je Vous Aime Beaucoup"
6. "I Love to Spend Each Evening with You"
7. "Moon River"
8. "Where the Blue of the Night"
9. "Blue Velvet"
10. "I'll Be Seeing You"

QUIZ #20 *(from page 34)*
1. Dean
2. Tony
3. Dean
4. Steve
5. Tony
6. Tony
7. Mary
8. Dean
9. Tony
10. Dean

QUIZ #21   *(from page 35)*

1. h
2. g
3. b
4. d
5. e
6. c
7. a
8. i
9. j
10. f

QUIZ #22   *(from page 37)*

1. Benny Goodman
2. Mariah Carey
3. Ralph Young
4. Carole King
5. Paul Whiteman
6. 1948
7. *The Godfather*
8. Frances Gumm
9. Glenn Miller
10. "Side by Side"

QUIZ #23   *(from page 39)*

1. Barry Alan Pincus
2. Brooklyn, New York
3. Accordion
4. Julliard
5. New York's Continental Bath House
6. Bette Midler
7. He wrote the jingles
8. Mandy
9. Memory
10. "I Write The Songs"

QUIZ #24 *(from page 41)*

1. a
2. c
3. a
4. b
5. c
6. a
7. c
8. a
9. c
10. b

QUIZ #25 *(from page 43)*

1. Maria
2. Marianne
3. Nancy
4. Matilda-Matilda
5. Mandy
6. Sue
7. Lydia-Lydia-Lydia
8. Alice
9. Peg
10. Margie-Margie

QUIZ #26 *(from page 44)*

1. g
2. d
3. c
4. a
5. h
6. f
7. b
8. j
9. e
10. i

QUIZ #27   *(from page 45)*

1. f
2. e
3. c
4. a
5. i
6. b
7. d
8. j
9. g
10. h

QUIZ #28   *(from page 47)*

1. McGuire Sisters
2. McGuire Sisters
3. Andrews Sisters
4. Andrews Sisters
5. McGuire Sisters
6. Andrews Sisters
7. McGuire Sisters
8. Andrews Sisters
9. McGuire Sisters
10. Andrews Sisters

QUIZ #29   *(from page 49)*

1. Fingers
2. Hair
3. Knee
4. Eyes-Eyes
5. Hands
6. Heart-Heart
7. Nose
8. Teeth
9. Thumb-Thumb
10. Fingers-Toes

QUIZ #30 *(from page 51)*

1. "Roses are Red"
2. Pat Boone
3. Betty Grable
4. 1959
5. "Music-Music-Music"
6. Anita Bryant
7. Les Brown
8. Dianne, Peggy, Kathy, Janet
9. Swing and Sway
10. Trumpet

QUIZ #31 *(from page 53)*

1. MacDonalds
2. Roto Rooter
3. Schlitz
4. Oscar Mayer
5. Good n' Plenty
6. State Farm
7. Bosco
8. Salem-Salem
9. Gillette
10. Wheaties

QUIZ #32 *(from page 54)*

1. h
2. g
3. b
4. j
5. c
6. d
7. e
8. i
9. a
10. f

QUIZ #33   *(from page 55)*

1. Tommy
2. Jimmy
3. Jimmy
4. Tommy
5. Tommy
6. Jimmy
7. Jimmy
8. Tommy
9. Tommy
10. Jimmy

QUIZ #34   *(from page 57)*

1. Joan
2. The Bon Soir
3. *I Can Get it for You Wholesale*
4. Elliot Gould
5. *Funny Girl*
6. Fanny Brice
7. "People"
8. *The Barbra Streisand Album*
9. *Yentl*
10. Neil Diamond

QUIZ #35   *(from page 59)*

1. e
2. g
3. a
4. c
5. b
6. d
7. h
8. j
9. i
10. f

QUIZ #36 *(from page 61)*
1. Oklahoma
2. Clara Ann Fowler
3. Mercury
4. "All My Love"
5. "Mockin' Bird Hill"
6. "Tennessee Waltz"
7. "I Went to Your Wedding"
8. "This Is My Song"
9. Benny Goodman
10. "Hush, Hush, Sweet Charlotte"

QUIZ #37 *(from page 62)*
1. Indiana
2. San Francisco
3. Avalon
4. Cape Cod
5. Mississippi
6. St. Louis, Louis
7. Ireland
8. New York, New York
9. Tennessee
10. Carolina

QUIZ #38 *(from page 63)*
1. Nellie
2. Suzie-Suzie
3. Irene-Irene
4. Amy-Amy
5. Paula
6. Dolly-Dolly
7. Ida
8. Margie-Margie
9. Linda
10. Mary-Mary

QUIZ #39   *(from page 65)*

1. e
2. d
3. g
4. j
5. i
6. b
7. f
8. c
9. h
10. a

QUIZ #40   *(from page 67)*

1. Drums
2. The Chordettes
3. Garth Brooks
4. Richard Whiting
5. Woody Guthrie
6. Sammy Kaye
7. Debbie Reynolds
8. The Four Freshmen
9. Coca-Cola
10. "A Very Precious Love"

QUIZ #41   *(from page 68)*

1. Lamb
2. Honey
3. Lemon
4. Wine
5. Apple
6. Cream-Coffee
7. Water
8. Sugar
9. Champagne
10. Cherries

QUIZ #42   *(from page 69)*

1. c
2. j
3. b
4. g
5. i
6. f
7. d
8. h
9. e
10. a

QUIZ #43   *(from page 71)*

1. c
2. a
3. a
4. b
5. b
6. c
7. a
8. b
9. a
10. c

QUIZ #44   *(from page 73)*

1. Autumn
2. Winter
3. Rain
4. Snow-Snow-Snow
5. Spring
6. Sunshine
7. Foggy
8. Stormy
9. Showers
10. Hazy-Summer

QUIZ #45 *(from page 75)*

1. Four Years Old
2. *Little Orphan Annie*
3. Chico Marx
4. The Mel-Tones
5. The Velvet Fog
6. "The Christmas Song"
7. Nat King Cole
8. *It Wasn't All Velvet*
9. *The Judy Garland Show*
10. *Night Court*

QUIZ #46 *(from page 76)*

1. Paris
2. Texas
3. Chicago
4. California
5. Pittsburgh-Pennsylvania
6. Russia
7. Ohio
8. Alabama
9. China-China
10. Vermont

QUIZ #47 *(from page 77)*

1. a
2. h
3. b
4. g
5. f
6. i
7. j
8. e
9. c
10. d

QUIZ #48 *(from page 79)*

1. Tom Jones
2. Engelbert Humperdinck
3. Engelbert Humperdinck
4. Tom Jones
5. Engelbert Humperdinck
6. Tom Jones
7. Tom Jones
8. Engelbert Humperdinck
9. Tom Jones
10. Engelbert Humperdinck

QUIZ #49 *(from page 81)*

1. Heart
2. Face
3. Heart-Heart
4. Hair
5. Feet
6. Skin
7. Eyes
8. Arms
9. Neck
10. Head-Shoulder

QUIZ #50 *(from page 83)*

1. Bob Hope
2. The Electric Guitar
3. Karen and Richard
4. Arthur Godfrey
5. "Too Much, Too Little, Too Late"
6. *Your Hit Parade*
7. Alice Lon
8. Arthur Tracy
9. Dinah Shore
10. Bill Kenny

QUIZ #51   *(from page 85)*

1. f
2. e
3. h
4. b
5. a
6. c
7. i
8. g
9. d
10. j

QUIZ #52   *(from page 87)*

1. Alfie
2. Harry
3. Popeye
4. Sam
5. Michael
6. Bill
7. Charlie, Charlie
8. Davey Crockett
9. Billie Joe
10. Norman, Norman

QUIZ #53   *(from page 89)*

1. The Mills Brothers
2. The Ink Spots
3. The Ink Spots
4. The Mills Brothers (John Sr. & John Jr.)
5. The Mills Brothers
6. The Ink Spots
7. The Ink Spots (Bill & Herbert Kenny)
8. The Ink Spots
9. The Mills Brothers
10. The Mills Brothers

QUIZ #54 *(from page 90)*

1. d
2. g
3. f
4. a
5. b
6. e
7. j
8. i
9. h
10. c

QUIZ #55 *(from page 91)*

1. c
2. j
3. e
4. i
5. a
6. h
7. b
8. g
9. d
10. f

QUIZ #56 *(from page 93)*

1. He was a broker
2. Ted Weems
3. Jo Stafford
4. RCA Victor
5. "Till the End of Time"
6. The Fontaine Sisters
7. Eddie Fisher
8. "Dream Along with Me"
9. "It's Impossible"
10. "Catch A Falling Star"

QUIZ #57   *(from page 95)*

1. "On the Street Where You Live"
2. Paul & Art
3. Carmen
4. Jimmy Dorsey
5. Glenn Miller
6. "Take Me Out to the Ballgame"
7. "Moon River"
8. The Kingston Trio
9. "I Am Woman"
10. *The Tonight Show* starring Johnny Carson

QUIZ #58   *(from page 97)*

1. e
2. a
3. c
4. h
5. d
6. f
7. b
8. g
9. j
10. i

QUIZ #59   *(from page 99)*

1. Gray
2. Green
3. Yellow
4. Pink
5. Red-Blue
6. Violets
7. White
8. Lemon
9. Brown-Blue
10. Brown-Yellow

QUIZ #60 *(from page 101)*

1. c
2. g
3. i
4. b
5. j
6. e
7. f
8. h
9. a
10. d

QUIZ #61 *(from page 103)*

1. Boxing
2. The 500 Club
3. *My Friend Irma*
4. *The Colgate Comedy Hour*
5. "That's Amore"
6. 1956
7. "Memories Are Made of This"
8. "Everybody Loves Somebody"
9. Matt Helm
10. Frank Sinatra, Sammy Davis, Jr., Peter Lawford, Shirley MacLaine

QUIZ #62 *(from page 105)*

1. The Modernaires
2. The Pied Pipers
3. The Pied Pipers
4. The Modernaires
5. The Pied Pipers
6. The Modernaires
7. The Pied Pipers
8. The Pied Pipers
9. The Modernaires
10. The Modernaires

QUIZ #63 *(from page 106)*

1. e
2. h
3. i
4. g
5. c
6. a
7. j
8. f
9. d
10. b

www.ingramcontent.com/pod-product-compliance
Lightning Source LLC
Chambersburg PA
CBHW070925270326
41927CB00011B/2727